SWITZERLAND T GUIDE 2025-2026:

Discover Scenic Wonders, Cultural Gems, Alpine Adventures, And Local Secrets

CAMDEN A. ROWE

Aerial view of Swiss Alps mountain ridge in summer

The turquoise waters of lake lungern (lungerersee) in obwalden, switzerland.

Switzerland Travel Guide 2025-2026

© Copyright 2025 by Camden A. Rowe. All rights reserved.

This document is designed to provide accurate and reliable information about the topic it covers, It is illegal to reproduce, copy, or share any part of this document, either electronically or in print. You are not allowed to record or store this document in any form without written permission from the publisher. This document is protected by copyright law.

Beautiful Swiss Alps Mountain Range In Switzerland.

Switzerland Travel Guide 2025-2026

TABLE OF CONTENTS

MAP OF SWITZERLAND — 5
INTRODUCTION — 7
   Why Visit Switzerland in 2025–2026? — 9
CHAPTER 1: OVERVIEW OF SWITZERLAND — 15
   Must-Know Facts for First-Time and Returning Travelers — 15
   Switzerland at a Glance: Climate, Geography & Regions — 17
   Interactive Maps and Regional Highlights — 19
   Travel Essentials by Region — 20
CHAPTER 2: A JOURNEY THROUGH TIME & TRADITION — 22
   A Brief History of Switzerland — 22
   Cultural Etiquette and Social Norms — 24
   Languages and Communication Tips — 24
   Swiss Traditions, Festivals, and Holidays — 26
   Art, Architecture, and Swiss Heritage — 27
CHAPTER 3: TRAVEL PLANNING & PREPARATION — 30
   Essential Documents and Visa Requirements — 30
   Travel Itinerary Planning Made Easy — 31
   Must-Pack Travel Kits: Essentials, Electronics & Safety — 32
   Travel Insurance: What You Need to Know — 34
   Currency, Exchange Tips, and Budgeting — 34
CHAPTER 4: GETTING AROUND SWITZERLAND — 36
   Transportation Overview: Trains, Trams, and Beyond — 36
   Using the Swiss Travel Pass & Regional Passes — 38
   Driving in Switzerland: Renting a Car or Camper — 40
   Domestic Flights and Scenic Rail Routes — 41
   Accessibility and Eco-Friendly Transit Options — 43
CHAPTER 5: WHERE TO STAY — 44
   Accommodation Types: Hotels, Chalets, Hostels, and Rentals — 44
   Budget-Friendly Stays: Value Without Sacrificing Comfort — 45
   Luxury Escapes: Top 5-Star Hotels and Spa Resorts — 48
   Family-Friendly Lodging and Group Options — 51
   Booking Tips, Local Platforms, and Hidden Gems — 53
CHAPTER 6: TASTE OF SWITZERLAND — 55
   Iconic Swiss Dishes You Must Try — 55
   Best Places to Eat: Local Cafés, Markets & Restaurants — 57
   Swiss Chocolate, Cheese, and Alpine Cuisine — 59
   Regional Food Specialties and Farm-to-Table Dining — 61
   Traveler Tips: Food Safety, Allergies & Etiquette — 63
CHAPTER 7: TOP DESTINATIONS & HIDDEN GEMS — 65

Switzerland Travel Guide 2025-2026

Zurich, Geneva, Lucerne & Bern: Urban Highlights	65
Interlaken, Zermatt & Jungfrau: Alpine Adventures	68
Lake Geneva, Montreux & Lausanne: Lakeside Beauty	70
Off-the-Beaten-Path Villages and Natural Wonders	72
UNESCO World Heritage Sites in Switzerland	73
CHAPTER 8: SMART TRAVEL TOOLS	**75**
Must-Have Travel Apps for Switzerland	75
SIM Cards, Roaming, and Wi-Fi Access	76
Emergency Contacts & Useful Swiss Helplines	77
Currency Converters, Train Schedulers & Translators	78
Tech Travel Tips: Charging, Adapters & Connectivity	79
CHAPTER 9:STAYING SAFE, CLEAN & INFORMED	**80**
Hygiene Standards and Public Facilities	80
Healthcare Access and Emergency Services	81
Travel Safety Tips and Common Laws to Know	83
Travel Scams to Avoid and How to Report Issues	84
Respecting Nature: Environmental Responsibility	85
CHAPTER 10: LIFE IN MOTION – SPORTS & MODERN SWITZERLAND	**87**
Popular Sports and Outdoor Activities	87
Current Events and Local Happenings (2025–2026)	89
Swiss Innovation and Modern Lifestyle	90
Volunteering, Working, and Extended Stay Tips	91
Engaging with Locals: Language, Respect & Cultural Exchange	92
CONCLUSION	**94**

Switzerland Travel Guide 2025-2026

MAP OF SWITZERLAND

Switzerland Travel Guide 2025-2026

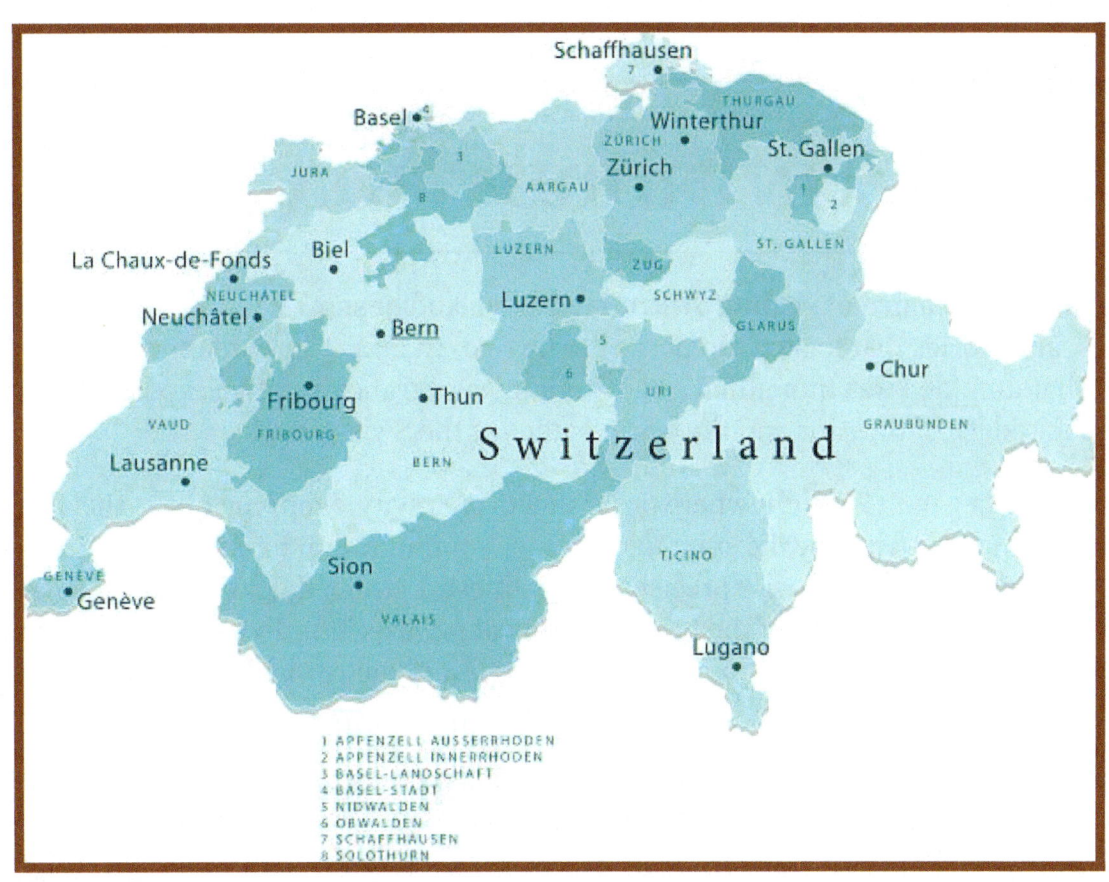

Switzerland Travel Guide 2025-2026

INTRODUCTION

I had always dreamed of visiting Switzerland—the land of snow-capped peaks, timeless trains, and stories that looked too perfect to be real. In 2025, that dream came to life, and what unfolded was more than a vacation; it was a transformative experience etched in the icy edges of the Alps and the warm smiles of the Swiss people.

My journey began in **Zurich**, where order meets creativity. Stepping out of the airport, I was immediately struck by the smooth efficiency—immigration took minutes, and trains were running on the dot, Swiss precision at its finest. I grabbed a Swiss Travel Pass, which turned out to be one of the best decisions of my trip. It unlocked access to trains, trams, buses, boats, and even some museum entries. If you're visiting, especially for the first time, get it—it saves both time and money.

Aerial view of Zurich, Switzerland

Zurich was vibrant yet composed, where cobbled alleys led to stylish cafes and old churches shared space with modern art galleries. I visited the **Kunsthaus Zürich** and

Switzerland Travel Guide 2025-2026

sipped hot chocolate at a riverside café while watching life unfold slowly along the Limmat River. But I knew the heart of Switzerland lay in its mountains, and so I journeyed on.

From Zurich, I took the **scenic Glacier Express**, dubbed the "slowest express train in the world," which winds its way through deep valleys, ancient bridges, and sleepy villages. The panoramic windows gave me an uninterrupted view of the Swiss countryside—rolling meadows, grazing cows with jingling bells, and sharp peaks that seemed to pierce the sky.

Zermatt town and Matterhorn mountain aerial panoramic view

I arrived in **Zermatt**, a car-free village nestled at the foot of the iconic **Matterhorn**. It felt like stepping into a snow globe. The silence was beautiful—no honking, no engines, just the crunch of snow underfoot and the distant laughter of skiers. I stayed at a cozy wooden chalet that smelled of pine and cinnamon, warmed by a crackling fireplace and welcoming hosts who served me raclette, a traditional Swiss cheese dish, and shared stories of mountain life.

My first attempt at skiing was humbling—I fell more times than I could count. But the instructors were patient, and by the third day, I could glide (albeit shakily) down a beginner's slope. The highlight came when I took the **Gornergrat Railway**, Europe's

Switzerland Travel Guide 2025-2026

highest open-air cogwheel train. From the summit, I saw the Matterhorn bathed in golden sunset light, surrounded by a sea of white peaks. It was one of those moments that take your breath away—not just because of the altitude.

After Zermatt, I made my way to **Lucerne**, often described as Switzerland's fairytale town. I crossed the **Chapel Bridge**, strolled the Old Town, and took a boat ride on **Lake Lucerne**, with snow-capped peaks reflected in crystal-clear waters. It was here I learned about Swiss neutrality during WWII, their multilingual culture (German, French, Italian, Romansh), and how respect, punctuality, and cleanliness are deeply embedded in their society.

Food was another adventure—beyond cheese and chocolate, I tried **Zürcher Geschnetzeltes** (sliced veal in creamy mushroom sauce), fresh pastries in Bern, and Alpine herbal teas in mountain lodges. Every region had its own flavors and stories.

One unexpected joy was how safe I felt, even when walking alone at night. Public toilets were spotless, tap water tasted better than bottled, and public transport announcements were accurate to the second. Even the cows seemed to follow a schedule!

What made Switzerland so memorable wasn't just its beauty—it was the harmony between nature and human ingenuity. The Swiss people didn't just build on the mountains—they worked with them. Their respect for the environment, commitment to sustainability, and multicultural inclusiveness impressed me deeply.

When I boarded my flight back, I looked one last time at the snowy Alps in the distance. Switzerland had shown me what it means to live with order, beauty, and balance. And though I was leaving, a part of me had found a new home in the stillness of its lakes and the rhythm of its trains.

I didn't just visit Switzerland. I experienced it—with heart, mind, and soul.

Why Visit Switzerland in 2025–2026?

1. Revamped Travel Infrastructure and Swiss Efficiency

Switzerland in 2025–2026 continues to set global benchmarks for transportation, sustainability, and traveler experience. The country's **public transport system has been enhanced** with:

- **Upgraded high-speed trains**, including new panoramic routes for sightseeing.

Switzerland Travel Guide 2025-2026

- **Green initiatives** in cable cars and buses to reduce carbon emissions.

- Digitalized travel networks, with **real-time multilingual apps** for scheduling, ticketing, and weather alerts.

Even first-time travelers can navigate effortlessly thanks to **streamlined immigration**, **modern airports**, and **automated transit hubs**. The Swiss Travel System remains one of the most punctual and interconnected in the world.

2. Switzerland's Global Events and Celebrations

2025–2026 is packed with **international festivals, exhibitions, and anniversaries**. Some major highlights include:

- **ExpoBern 2025** – A global innovation and sustainability expo drawing thinkers and tourists alike.

- **Montreux Jazz Festival (2025 & 2026 editions)** – A world-famous music festival on the banks of Lake Geneva.

- **Swiss National Day (August 1st)** – A cultural deep dive into fireworks, alphorns, and local parades in every canton.

- **UNESCO heritage exhibitions** – Celebrating Swiss contributions to world culture, hosted across Geneva, Lausanne, and Lucerne.

These events make 2025–2026 an ideal time to experience Switzerland in full cultural bloom.

3. Safer and Smarter Travel Post-Pandemic

Switzerland has become a **beacon of post-pandemic recovery**, with:

- **Advanced health monitoring at borders and airports.**

- **Digital health passports** and multilingual support for travelers.

- **Sanitation upgrades** in hotels, trains, and public spaces.
- Comprehensive **travel insurance partnerships** integrated into booking systems.

Switzerland Travel Guide 2025-2026

Travelers in 2025–2026 can enjoy peace of mind knowing **health safety protocols are world-class** while still experiencing freedom and spontaneity.

4. Cutting-Edge Eco-Tourism and Sustainability

Switzerland's commitment to green travel is more visible than ever:

- **Carbon-neutral lodges** and eco-villages in the Alps.
- **Electric boat rides** across Lake Lucerne and Lake Geneva.
- Guided **wildlife and glacier preservation tours**.
- Hiking trails with **QR code storytelling panels** about local ecology.

With **75% of energy now renewable**, traveling through Switzerland allows visitors to **enjoy luxury and nature responsibly.**

5. New Attractions and Timeless Wonders

In addition to classic landmarks like the **Matterhorn, Jungfrau**, and **Château de Chillon**, 2025–2026 introduces several exciting additions:

World famous mountain peak Matterhorn above Zermatt town, Switzerland

Switzerland Travel Guide 2025-2026

- **The Lucerne SkyDeck** – A new high-altitude observation platform with VR experiences.

- **Alpine Adventure Parks** – Family-friendly eco-resorts blending hiking, history, and hospitality.

- **Updated museum exhibits** using AI-guided tours and immersive reality.

Timeless experiences such as **the Glacier Express, chocolate tasting in Broc**, and **watchmaking tours in Geneva** remain as magical as ever, but now with enhanced services and multilingual options.

6. Ideal for Every Type of Traveler

Switzerland in 2025–2026 caters to every travel style:

- **Solo travelers:** Safe cities, efficient transport, and vibrant youth hostels.

- **Couples:** Romantic lakeside towns like Montreux and Lucerne.

- **Families:** Child-friendly attractions like Swiss Miniatur and Heidi Village.

- **Adventure seekers:** Glacier trekking, paragliding in Interlaken, and summer skiing in Saas-Fee.

- **Luxury travelers:** 5-star chalets, spa resorts, and private train cabins.

Whether you're planning a quiet escape or a full-throttle alpine adventure, Switzerland offers **a perfectly balanced mix of nature, culture, and convenience.**

7. Political Stability and Economic Strength

Few countries offer the **level of political neutrality, cleanliness, and organization** that Switzerland does. In 2025–2026, its:

- **Stable economy**

- **Low crime rate**

- **Efficient legal systems**

Switzerland Travel Guide 2025-2026

- And **citizen-centric governance**

make it an ideal destination for travelers looking for **reliability and order** amidst global uncertainties.

8. Authentic Cultural Immersion

Switzerland is not just a destination; it's a collection of **multilingual, multicultural regions**. In 2025–2026, there is increased focus on:

- **Local homestays and village experiences**.

- Language-learning tours (French in Vaud, German in Lucerne, Italian in Ticino).

Landscape of Lugano lake, mountains and the city located below, Ticino, Switzerland

- **Alpine farming and cheese-making workshops**.

- Folk dance events and heritage storytelling evenings.

Travelers can now go beyond sightseeing and become **active participants in Swiss traditions.**

Switzerland Travel Guide 2025-2026

CHAPTER 1: OVERVIEW OF SWITZERLAND

Must-Know Facts for First-Time and Returning Travelers

Language

Switzerland has **four national languages**:

- **German** (spoken by around 65% – mostly in the central and eastern parts)
- **French** (in the west: Geneva, Lausanne, Montreux)

Geneva skyline cityscape, French-Swiss in Switzerland

Switzerland Travel Guide 2025-2026

- **Italian** (mainly in the south, Ticino)

- **Romansh** (spoken by a tiny population in parts of Graubünden)

Most Swiss speak **English very well**, especially in cities, train stations, and hotels. Still, learning a few basic phrases in German or French will go a long way.

Currency

- The **Swiss Franc (CHF)** is the official currency. Euros are accepted in some tourist areas but usually at **unfavorable exchange rates**.

Swiss Franc

- 1 CHF ≈ **1.12 USD** (as of June 2025)
- Cards are widely accepted, even at mountain huts. But it's wise to carry **some cash for rural areas** or small bakeries.

Time Zone

- Switzerland follows **Central European Time (CET)**: UTC +1

- **Daylight saving time** is observed (UTC +2 from late March to late October)

Switzerland Travel Guide 2025-2026

Power Plugs

- Plug type **J** (three-prong, Swiss-specific)
- Voltage: **230V / 50Hz**
- Bring a **universal adapter**; many hotel rooms have multi-socket options.

Emergency Numbers

- Police: **117**
- Ambulance: **144**
- Fire: **118**
- European emergency: **112**

Tipping

Tipping is **not mandatory**—service charges are included in bills. But rounding up or leaving **5–10% at restaurants** for great service is appreciated.

Switzerland at a Glance: Climate, Geography & Regions

Climate

Switzerland's weather is surprisingly diverse for such a small country.

- **Summer (June–August):** 18–28°C (64–82°F). Perfect for hiking, lake swimming, and open-air festivals.
- **Autumn (September–November):** 8–18°C (46–64°F). Fewer crowds and golden alpine views.
- **Winter (December–February):** -5–5°C (23–41°F). Snowfall blankets ski towns like Zermatt, St. Moritz, and Davos.

View of St. Moritz

- **Spring (March–May):** 10–20°C (50–68°F). Wildflowers, waterfalls, and the return of green trails.

👉 **Tip:** Weather can shift rapidly in the Alps. Always carry **layers, waterproof gear, and sunblock**, even in summer.

Geography & Regions

Switzerland is split into **three major geographical regions**, each with its own vibe:

- **The Alps (South & East):** Iconic peaks, snow sports, and traditional alpine villages. Think **Zermatt, Grindelwald, Davos, and St. Moritz**.

- **The Central Plateau (Midland):** Urban centers like **Zurich, Bern, and Lucerne**, rolling countryside, lakes, and high-speed rail lines.

- **The Jura (Northwest):** Less-traveled, forested hills, watchmaking heritage, and great hiking—**Neuchâtel and Jura canton** are highlights.

Switzerland Travel Guide 2025-2026

Regional Highlights

- **German-speaking region:** Zurich, Lucerne, Interlaken – clean, organized, and full of mountain access points.

Aerial Panorama of the Old Town medieval architecture in Lucerne, Switzerland

- **French-speaking region:** Geneva, Lausanne, Montreux – lakeside beauty, wine culture, and elegant city life.

- **Italian-speaking region:** Lugano, Locarno – Mediterranean vibes, palm trees, and piazza cafés.

- **Romansh-speaking region:** Scuol, Samedan – lesser-known but incredibly authentic.

Interactive Maps and Regional Highlights

For planning your route or just exploring by interest, use the following **official interactive maps** and travel planners:

Switzerland Travel Guide 2025-2026

🗺 Swiss Travel Map

The best place to start. Zoom into any canton, town, or mountain hut, and see what's nearby.
🔗 www.myswitzerland.com/map

📕 SBB Travel Planner

Switzerland's national rail service. Plan train and bus routes, view real-time updates, and buy tickets directly.
🔗 www.sbb.ch/en
💰 Swiss Travel Pass: CHF 262 for 3 days (2nd class), includes boats, museums, and panoramic trains.

🔺 Hiking and Trail Map

Interactive trail maps with altitude, weather, difficulty level, and recommended gear.
🔗 www.schweizmobil.ch

🛶 Swiss Lakes & Outdoor Guide

Ideal for exploring summer sports, scenic lakes, and outdoor routes.
🔗 www.outdooractive.com

Travel Essentials by Region

Here's a quick **breakdown of regional highlights** every traveler should consider:

Zurich Region

- **Must-see:** Old Town, Kunsthaus Museum, Lake Zurich promenade
- **Good to know:** Zurich is Switzerland's financial hub but offers incredible nature within 20 minutes of the city
- **Hotel range:** CHF 120–500/night
- **Local tip:** Get a **Zurich Card** (CHF 27/day) for museums and unlimited public transit

Bernese Oberland

- **Must-see:** Lauterbrunnen Valley, Jungfraujoch (Top of Europe), Grindelwald
- **Activities:** Paragliding, glacier hikes, cable cars

Switzerland Travel Guide 2025-2026

- **Hotel range:** CHF 90–400/night
- **Pro tip:** Stay in **Wengen** or **Mürren** if you prefer car-free alpine villages

Lake Geneva Region

- **Must-see:** Chillon Castle, Montreux, vineyards of Lavaux
- **Culture:** French influence, lakeside jazz, wine tasting
- **Hotel range:** CHF 100–600/night
- **Don't miss:** GoldenPass panoramic train from Montreux to Zweisimmen

Ticino (Italian-speaking south)

- **Must-see:** Lugano, Verzasca Valley, Bellinzona castles

Castelgrande, one of Bellinzonas Castles, Unesco World, Heritage in Switzerland

- **Climate:** Mild winters, palm trees, lakeside beaches
- **Hotel range:** CHF 80–350/night
- **Travel tip:** Try the **Gotthard Panorama Express** (boat + train) for scenic lake-to-mountain transition

Switzerland Travel Guide 2025-2026

CHAPTER 2: A JOURNEY THROUGH TIME & TRADITION

A Brief History of Switzerland

Switzerland may be famous for chocolate and clocks, but its history runs deep—and it's anything but boring.

- **1291: The Birth of the Swiss Confederation**
  Switzerland began when three alpine regions—**Uri, Schwyz, and Unterwalden**—pledged mutual defense against invading powers. This pact laid the foundation for what would become the **Swiss Confederation**.

Schwyz town in Alps mountains, Central Switzerland, on a summer day

Switzerland Travel Guide 2025-2026

- **1515: Embracing Neutrality**
  After a crushing defeat at the **Battle of Marignano**, Switzerland adopted a policy of **perpetual neutrality**—a principle it still holds. It has stayed out of both World Wars and remains politically neutral today.

- **1848: A Modern Federal State**
  After a brief civil conflict, Switzerland became a **federal republic**, with a constitution that blended **central government and strong local cantonal autonomy**.

- **2002: Joins the United Nations**
  Despite its global influence, Switzerland only joined the UN in 2002, emphasizing its cautious, independent approach to international affairs.

📍 **Swiss National Museum, Zurich**
Learn the full timeline of Swiss evolution in this beautifully curated museum.
🎟 Entry: CHF 10
🔗 www.landesmuseum.ch

National Museum Zurich

Switzerland Travel Guide 2025-2026

Cultural Etiquette and Social Norms

Swiss society is grounded in **politeness, discretion, and punctuality**. It's not flashy, but it runs like clockwork.

■ Do:

- **Be on time**. Trains, meetings, dinners—**punctuality is sacred**.

- **Greet with a firm handshake**, and in smaller towns, expect a **three-kiss greeting (alternating cheeks)** among friends.

- Say **"Grüezi"** (hello in German-speaking areas), **"Bonjour"** (French), or **"Buongiorno"** (Italian).

- Use **formal titles (Herr, Madame)** until invited otherwise.

✗ Don't:

- Don't make loud phone calls in public spaces.

- Don't litter—Switzerland takes cleanliness very seriously.

- Don't interrupt. Swiss conversations are polite and turn-based.

Dress modestly, especially in small towns or churches. Even in casual settings, the Swiss lean toward **neat and tidy** over flashy.

Languages and Communication Tips

Switzerland is like **four countries in one** when it comes to language.

● Official Languages by Region:

- **German** – Zurich, Lucerne, Bern, Basel

- **French** – Geneva, Lausanne, Montreux

Switzerland Travel Guide 2025-2026

- **Italian** – Lugano, Locarno, Bellinzona

Scenic cityscape of Lugano

- **Romansh** – Only in some areas of Graubünden (spoken by under 1%)

Even though street signs may differ by region, most people—especially in tourism—**speak very good English**.

Useful Tools:

- **Google Translate**: works well offline.
- **SayHi Translate**: for real-time conversation.
- **Linguarena (Swiss German app)** – great if you want to break the ice in Zürich or Bern.

www.linguarena.ch

Tip: Learn a few key words like:

- "Bitte" (please)
- "Merci" (thank you, in both French and Swiss German)
- "Wo ist…?" (Where is…?)

Switzerland Travel Guide 2025-2026

- "Ein Bier, bitte" (just in case you end up in a brewery tour)

Swiss Traditions, Festivals, and Holidays

Switzerland has a rich blend of rural traditions and big-city festivals. While some events are tourist-friendly, many are deeply local and culturally rooted.

🎉 **Top Annual Festivals:**

- **Fête de l'Escalade** (Geneva – December): Celebrates the city's defense against a 1602 invasion. Locals dress in period costumes and drink hot chocolate.
  🔗 www.escalade.ch

Tehe Sechseläuten

- **Sechseläuten** (Zurich – April): A symbolic burning of the "Böögg" snowman to predict summer weather.
  🎬 Free to watch – parades and fanfare around the city.
  🔗 www.sechselaeuten.ch
- **Montreux Jazz Festival** (July): One of Europe's best-known music festivals, hosted by Lake Geneva.
  🎬 From CHF 50–300, depending on the act.
  🔗 www.montreuxjazzfestival.com

Switzerland Travel Guide 2025-2026

- **Alpabfahrt / Désalpe** (September – nationwide): Cows are paraded down the mountains after summer grazing, decorated with flowers and bells. Expect cheese stalls and brass bands.

🪧 **Public Holidays to Know:**

- **August 1 – Swiss National Day**
- **Easter Weekend (Good Friday to Easter Monday)**
- **Christmas (December 25–26)**

Many small shops and restaurants close on holidays, so **plan ahead**—especially in rural areas.

Art, Architecture, and Swiss Heritage

Switzerland may be known for natural beauty, but its **cultural depth** is just as fascinating.

🖼 Art & Museums

Kunsthaus Zürich

Switzerland Travel Guide 2025-2026

- **Kunsthaus Zürich** – Swiss and international art, from medieval to contemporary.
  - 🎞 CHF 23 entry
  - 🔗 www.kunsthaus.ch

- **Fondation Beyeler (Basel)** – Modern art lovers will appreciate works by Monet, Rothko, and Picasso.
  - 🎞 CHF 25
  - 🔗 www.fondationbeyeler.ch

- **Paul Klee Center (Bern)** – Dedicated to the abstract genius and Swiss-German artist.
  - 🎞 CHF 20
  - 🔗 www.zpk.org

Center of Paul Klee in Bern, Switzerland

🏰 Architecture & Heritage

- **Château de Chillon (Montreux)** – A fairytale lakeside castle that's one of Switzerland's most visited monuments.

Switzerland Travel Guide 2025-2026

- CHF 13.50
- www.chillon.ch

- **Abbey of Saint Gall** – A UNESCO World Heritage Site with a stunning baroque library.
    - CHF 18
    - www.stibi.ch

Abbey of Saint Gall in Switzerland

- **Old Towns** – Wander through **Lucerne**, **Stein am Rhein**, or **Gruyères**, where cobbled streets and timbered houses preserve medieval charm.

Tip: Swiss museums are often **free with the Swiss Travel Pass**, and many are **closed on Mondays**.

CHAPTER 3: TRAVEL PLANNING & PREPARATION

Essential Documents and Visa Requirements

Switzerland is part of the **Schengen Area**, which means a **Schengen visa** is required for non-EU/EEA nationals from many countries. Here's what you'll need:

✈ **Required Documents:**

- **Passport** (valid for at least **3 months beyond your departure date**)
- **Return or onward ticket**
- **Proof of accommodation** (hotel bookings or invitation letter)
- **Travel insurance** covering at least **€30,000** in medical expenses
- **Bank statements or proof of sufficient funds**

■ **Visa-Free Countries:**

If you're from the **US, UK, Canada, Australia, New Zealand, Japan, or most EU countries**, you can stay **up to 90 days in any 180-day period** visa-free.

📌 Schengen Visa Application Info:

- Fee: **€80 (approx. CHF 75)**
- Processing time: **15–20 days**
- Apply via Swiss embassy or consulate in your country
  🔗 www.eda.admin.ch/visa

Switzerland Travel Guide 2025-2026

Travel Itinerary Planning Made Easy

Planning a trip to Switzerland doesn't have to be overwhelming. Whether you're chasing mountain views or lakeside calm, consider these essentials when building your route.

🍡 **Suggested 7-Day Itinerary** *(great for first-timers):*

- **Day 1:** Arrive in Zurich, explore Old Town

- **Day 2–3:** Lucerne + Mt. Pilatus or Mt. Rigi

Mount Pilatus

- **Day 4–5:** Interlaken & Lauterbrunnen Valley

- **Day 6:** Zermatt & Gornergrat

- **Day 7:** Geneva or return to Zurich

Tip: The **Swiss Travel Pass** simplifies everything—unlimited train, bus, and boat rides plus free entry to 500+ museums.
🎞 Prices: CHF 262 (3 days), CHF 418 (8 days)
🔗 www.swisstravelsystem.com

Switzerland Travel Guide 2025-2026

🎒 **Tools for Planning:**

- **SBB App** – Plan routes, buy tickets, see live train updates
- **Rome2Rio** – Compare transport options between towns
- **Komoot / AllTrails** – For hikers looking for mountain trail guides

Must-Pack Travel Kits: Essentials, Electronics & Safety

Suitcase packed Travel Essential

Switzerland is safe and well-equipped, but being prepared helps you explore without hiccups.

🎒 **Essentials:**

- **Passport** + copies
- **Swiss Travel Pass or Half Fare Card**

Switzerland Travel Guide 2025-2026

- **Travel-size toiletries** (though most are available in Swiss pharmacies)

- **Reusable water bottle** – tap water is crystal-clear and drinkable

- **Good walking shoes** – cobbled streets and mountain trails await

🔌 **Electronics:**

- **Universal power adapter** (Type J, 230V)

- **Portable charger** – trains often have USB outlets, but not always

- **Offline maps app** or screenshots in case of signal drops in rural areas

🧴 **Safety Items:**

- **Small first aid kit** – especially for hikers

- **Personal ID and emergency contacts** in wallet

- **A lightweight daypack** with anti-theft zippers if using public transport in cities

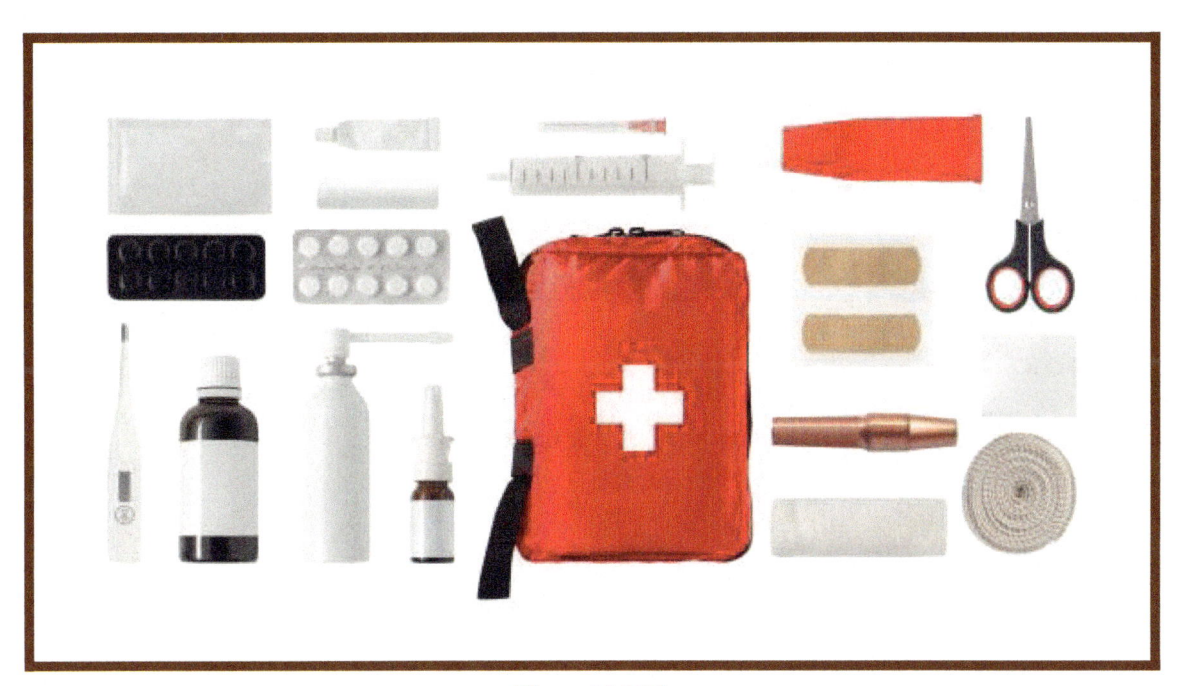

First Aid Kit

Tip: Keep all valuables in a **front-facing bag** when in busy places like train stations.

Switzerland Travel Guide 2025-2026

Travel Insurance: What You Need to Know

Don't skip this. Swiss healthcare is excellent but **expensive if you're uninsured**.

🛡 **Coverage Checklist:**

- **Emergency medical treatment** (minimum €30,000)
- **Accidents and injury** (especially if skiing, hiking, or paragliding)
- **Trip cancellation/delay**
- **Baggage loss or theft**

▪ **Recommended Providers:**

- **World Nomads** – Great for adventure travelers
  🔗 www.worldnomads.com

- **SafetyWing** – Flexible coverage, great for longer stays
  🔗 www.safetywing.com

- **Allianz Travel** – Well-known, solid global coverage
  🔗 www.allianztravelinsurance.com

▪ Expect to pay around **CHF 40–80** for a one-week trip, depending on coverage.

Currency, Exchange Tips, and Budgeting

💰 **Currency Info:**

- **Swiss Franc (CHF)** – Not part of the Eurozone
- **Coins:** 5, 10, 20, 50 Rappen; 1, 2, 5 CHF
- **Bills:** 10, 20, 50, 100, 200, 1000 CHF

▪ **Payments:**

- Credit/debit cards widely accepted
- Contactless works everywhere from **bakeries to gondolas**
- Some mountain huts and rural shops may ask for **cash (Bargeld)**

Switzerland Travel Guide 2025-2026

💱 **Best Exchange Tips:**

- **Avoid airport kiosks** – worst rates

- Use ATMs like **UBS, PostFinance, or Raiffeisen**

The Raiffeisen bank branch ATM in Viara Gambarogno, district of Locarno.

- Or use travel cards like **Wise** or **Revolut** for real-time exchange rates

🧾 **Budgeting Breakdown (Daily average per person):**

- **Budget travel:** CHF 80–120
  (Hostels, street food, public transport)

- **Mid-range:** CHF 150–250
  (3-star hotels, sit-down meals, scenic trains)

- **Luxury:** CHF 300+
  (Boutique stays, fine dining, private transfers)

Switzerland Travel Guide 2025-2026

CHAPTER 4: GETTING AROUND SWITZERLAND

Transportation Overview: Trains, Trams, and Beyond

Switzerland's public transportation system is one of the best in the world—**clean, efficient, scenic**, and it runs with a level of punctuality that borders on obsessive.

📖 Trains (SBB/CFF/FFS)

Sign of Swiss Federal Railways at Bern train station

- Swiss Federal Railways (**SBB**, known as **CFF** in French and **FFS** in Italian) connects **every major city and village**.

Switzerland Travel Guide 2025-2026

35

- Trains are frequent and comfortable, with **free Wi-Fi on most intercity lines**.

- Popular scenic routes like the **Glacier Express** and **Bernina Express** are national treasures.

Glacier Express

🎟 Ticket Prices:

- Zurich to Lucerne: CHF 25 (2nd class, one-way)

- Geneva to Interlaken: CHF 68
  🔗 www.sbb.ch/en

🚊 Trams & Buses

- In cities like **Zurich, Basel, Bern, and Geneva**, trams are the lifeblood of daily life.

- **Tickets must be validated** before boarding (unless you use an app or travel pass).

Switzerland Travel Guide 2025-2026

- Schedules run like clockwork, and connections are tightly coordinated.

📱 Use the **SBB Mobile** app or **Citymapper** to navigate city transport effortlessly.

🚤 **Boats**

- Ferries and boats cruise across lakes like **Lake Geneva, Lake Lucerne**, and **Lake Zurich**.

Vineyards and panorama on Lake Geneva

- Boat rides are not just transport—they're an experience, often included with travel passes.

Using the Swiss Travel Pass & Regional Passes

If you plan to move around the country a lot, the **Swiss Travel Pass** is your golden ticket.

🎟 Swiss Travel Pass

- Unlimited travel on trains, buses, boats, and trams nationwide

Switzerland Travel Guide 2025-2026

- Includes free admission to **500+ museums**, plus discounted or free entry to mountain cable cars

● **Valid for 3, 4, 6, 8 or 15 days**
💰 Prices (2nd class):

- 3 days: CHF 262

- 8 days: CHF 418
  🔗 www.swisstravelsystem.com

Tip: It includes iconic scenic trains like the **Bernina Express** and **GoldenPass Line**, but **seat reservations (CHF 10–49) are separate**.

Bernina-Express Railway, Graubünden, Switzerland

🎒 Regional Passes

If you're staying in one area, a **regional pass** may save you more:

- **Berner Oberland Pass** – CHF 250 for 4 days, covers Interlaken, Lauterbrunnen, Grindelwald
  🔗 www.regionalpass-berneroberland.ch

Switzerland Travel Guide 2025-2026

- **Tell-Pass (Central Switzerland)** – CHF 190 for 3 days, includes Lucerne and Mt. Pilatus cable cars
  🔗 www.tellpass.ch

Overhead cable car to the top of Mount Pilatus in Canton Lucerne, Switzerland

Driving in Switzerland: Renting a Car or Camper

While public transport is top-notch, driving gives you freedom—especially in the **Valais, Ticino, and Jura** regions where connections are less frequent.

🚗 Rental Cars

- You must be **18+** (sometimes 21) and hold a valid license (an **International Driving Permit** is advised if your license isn't in English, German, French or Italian).
- **Automatic cars are limited**—book early if you prefer one.
- Winter tires and **vignettes (CHF 40 highway sticker)** are mandatory (usually included in rental).

💰 Average cost: CHF 60–100/day
🚗 Top agencies: Europcar, Hertz, Sixt
🔗 www.autoeurope.eu

Switzerland Travel Guide 2025-2026

🏕 Campers & Motorhomes

- Ideal for slow travel or if you're chasing lakes and valleys.
- Campsites are well-equipped but **wild camping is restricted** (only allowed with landowner's permission).

🔗 Rentals: www.campanda.com, www.mycamper.ch

⬛ **Note:** Parking is limited and expensive in cities—**avoid driving in Zurich, Geneva, or Bern** unless absolutely necessary.

Bern, Switzerland with the clock tower at dawn

Domestic Flights and Scenic Rail Routes

✈ Domestic Flights

- Switzerland is small—**domestic flights aren't necessary** and are rare.
- From Geneva to Zurich, flying takes longer door-to-door than the **high-speed train (2h 45min)**.

⬢ **Skip flying** inside Switzerland unless connecting internationally.

Switzerland Travel Guide 2025-2026

🎒 Scenic Train Routes

These panoramic rides are among Switzerland's top attractions:

- **Glacier Express (Zermatt to St. Moritz)**
  Duration: 8 hours of pure alpine magic
  🎟️ Reservation: CHF 49 + Swiss Travel Pass or ticket
  🔗 www.glacierexpress.ch
- **Bernina Express (Chur to Tirano, Italy)**
  A UNESCO-listed ride over 196 bridges
  🎟️ Reservation: CHF 20–26
  🔗 www.rhb.ch/en

Scenery from GoldenPass Line - Brunig Pass in autumn

- **GoldenPass Line (Lucerne to Montreux)**
  Lake views, cow pastures, and vineyard slopes all in one day
  🎟️ Free with Swiss Travel Pass, reserve panoramic seats (CHF 8–15)
  🔗 www.goldenpassline.ch

Switzerland Travel Guide 2025-2026

Accessibility and Eco-Friendly Transit Options

Switzerland is not just beautiful—it's **inclusive and sustainable** too.

■ Accessibility

- Most major train stations and city buses are **wheelchair accessible**.
- SBB offers **free assistance** for travelers with mobility issues—book **1 hour in advance**.
  🔗 www.sbb.ch/en/assistance
- Popular hiking destinations like **Mt. Rigi** and **Jungfraujoch** offer step-free access and elevators.

Aerial view jungfraujoch

🌱 Eco-Friendly Tips

- Use **e-bikes** in cities like Lausanne and Basel (rented via PubliBike – from CHF 0.25/min)
  🔗 www.publibike.ch
- Stay in **Swiss Green Label hotels**, which commit to environmental standards.
  🔗 www.swisstainable.ch
- Choose **train over car or plane** for the lowest carbon footprint—it's part of the Swiss way of life.

Switzerland Travel Guide 2025-2026

CHAPTER 5: WHERE TO STAY

Accommodation Types: Hotels, Chalets, Hostels, and Rentals

Switzerland offers a wide range of places to rest your head, from **historic lakefront hotels** to **wooden chalets tucked in snowy valleys**. Prices can swing high, but there are great options at every level—if you know where to look.

🏨 Hotels

- Found everywhere from mountain villages to major cities.
- Standard amenities: **free Wi-Fi**, **breakfast buffet**, and **spotless rooms**.
- Most hotels charge a **city tax (CHF 2–5/night)**—not included in the room rate.

🔍 Use www.myswitzerland.com to find and compare Swiss Tourism-certified hotels.

🏠 Chalets & Alpine Lodges

- Best in **Grindelwald, Zermatt, Davos**, and **Saas-Fee**.
- Many are **self-catering**, perfect for families or longer stays.
- Some offer **half-board with local cuisine**, and a warm wooden interior that feels like home.

💰 Prices: CHF 100–600+/night depending on size and view.

🛏 Hostels

- Switzerland's hostels are clean, modern, and often in incredible locations.

Switzerland Travel Guide 2025-2026

- Look for **Swiss Youth Hostels** — great value and family-friendly.
  🔗 www.youthhostel.ch

💰 Prices: CHF 35–60 for dorm beds, CHF 90–130 for private rooms.

🏠 **Apartments & Short-Term Rentals**

- Great for groups or travelers who want to **cook their own meals**.

- Found on **Booking.com**, **Airbnb**, or **e-domizil.ch**.

- Be mindful of **cleaning fees** and **minimum stays**, especially during ski season.

<u>Budget-Friendly Stays: Value Without Sacrificing Comfort</u>

You don't need to blow your budget to enjoy a clean, cozy place in Switzerland.

🏠 **Best Budget Picks by Region:**

Hotel Marta, Zurich

Switzerland Travel Guide 2025-2026

44

- **Zurich** – *Hotel Marta* (Modern, near Old Town, free breakfast)
    - 💰 CHF 130–150/night
    - 🔗 www.hotelmarta.ch

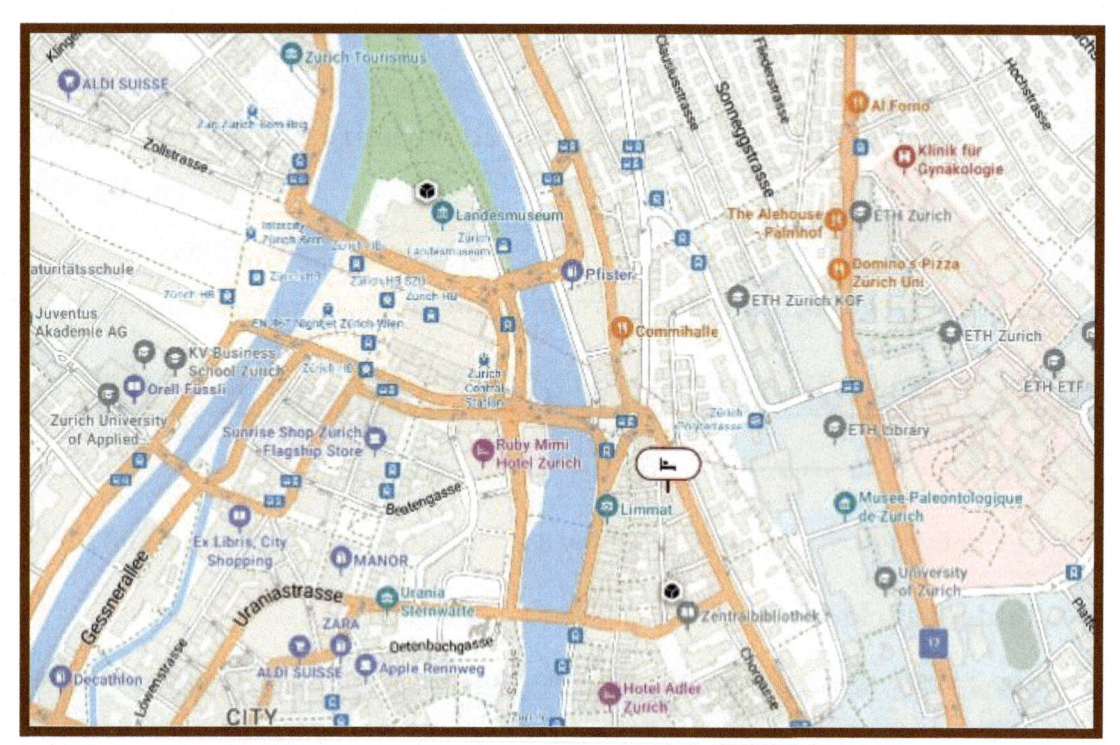

Map Showing Hotel Marta, Zurich and it's Vicinity

- **Lucerne** – *Barabas Hotel* (former prison turned hip hostel-hotel)
    - 💰 Dorms from CHF 45, doubles from CHF 110
    - 🔗 www.barabas-luzern.ch

- **Interlaken** – *Backpackers Villa Sonnenhof* (includes guest card & kitchen access)
    - 💰 Dorms from CHF 40, privates from CHF 95
    - 🔗 www.villa.ch

- **Geneva** – *City Hostel Geneva* (near train station, includes transit card)
    - 💰 CHF 50–80 per bed
    - 🔗 www.cityhostel.ch

Switzerland Travel Guide 2025-2026

City Hostel Geneva

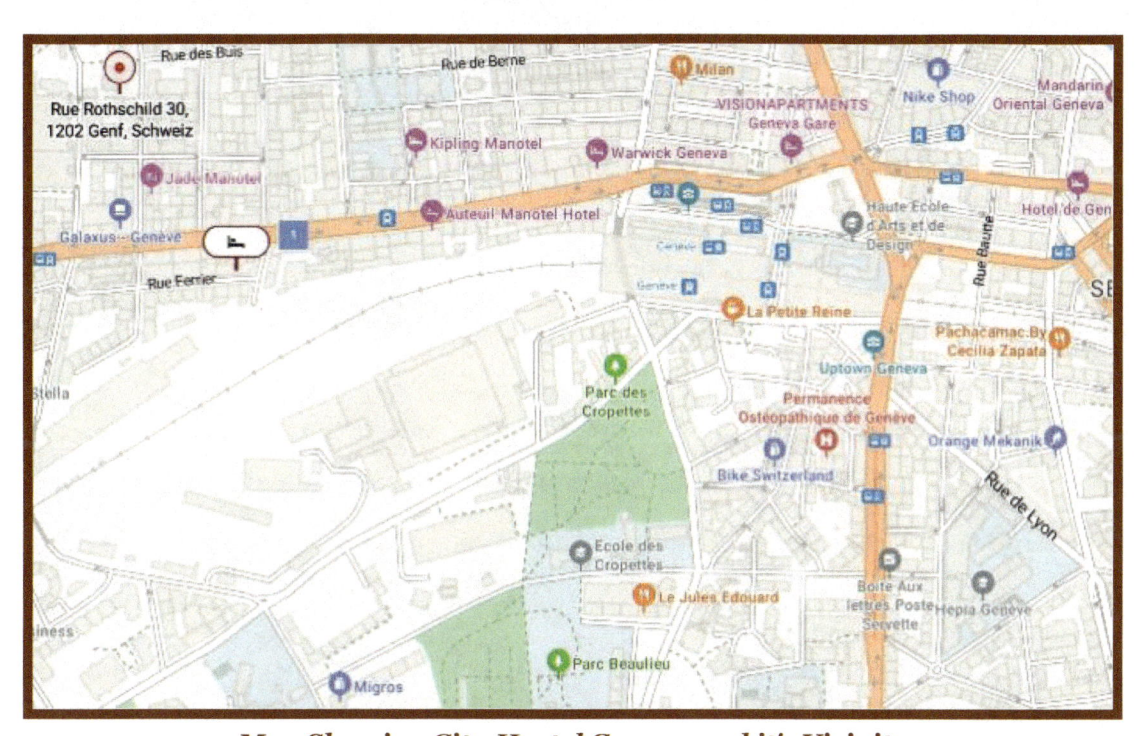

Map Showing City Hostel Geneva and it's Vicinity

🎙 **Budget Tip:** Look for properties offering the **local guest card** (e.g. Bern Ticket, Geneva Transport Card) for **free public transport and discounts**.

Switzerland Travel Guide 2025-2026

Luxury Escapes: Top 5-Star Hotels and Spa Resorts

For travelers seeking indulgence, Switzerland knows how to deliver. Think **mountain-view spas, Michelin-starred dining**, and top-tier Swiss service.

🔺 Top Luxury Hotels to Bookmark:

- **Badrutt's Palace, St. Moritz** – Iconic, glam, and snowy-chic
  💰 From CHF 800/night
  🔗 www.badruttspalace.com

Badrutt's Palace, Hotel, St. Moritz

Switzerland Travel Guide 2025-2026

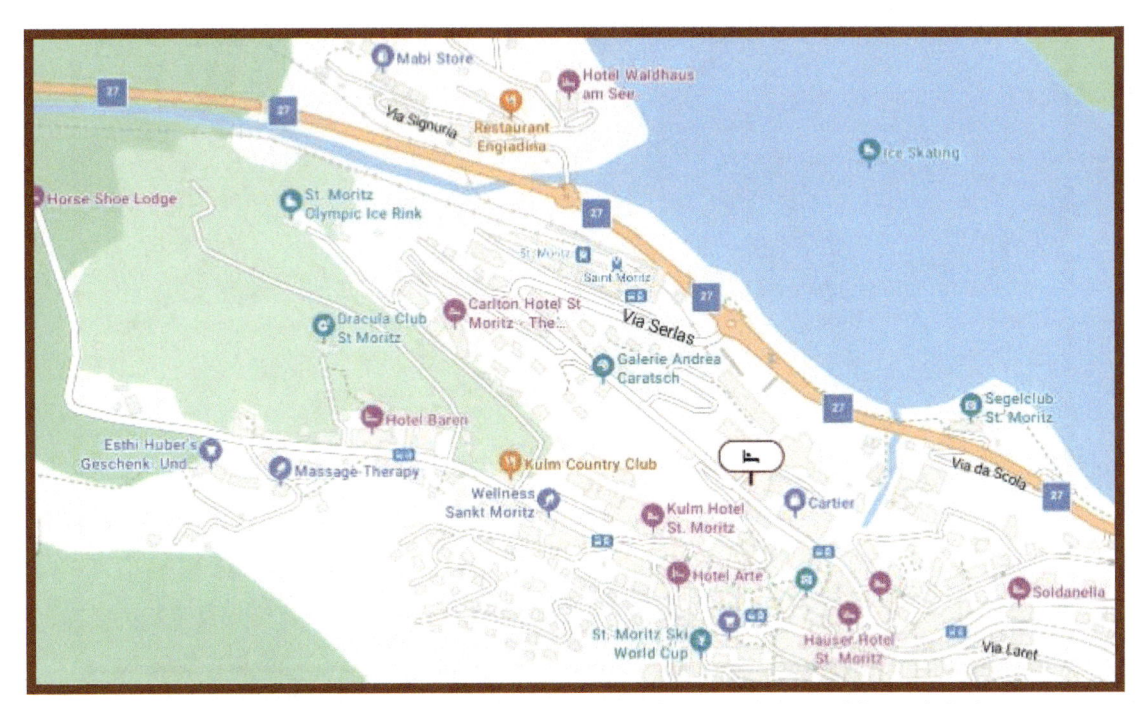

Map Showing Badrutt's Palace Hotel, St. Moritz and it's Vicinity

- **The Chedi, Andermatt** – Asian-Swiss fusion design, world-class spa
  💰 From CHF 700/night
  🔗 www.thechediandermatt.com

The Chedi, Andermatt

Switzerland Travel Guide 2025-2026

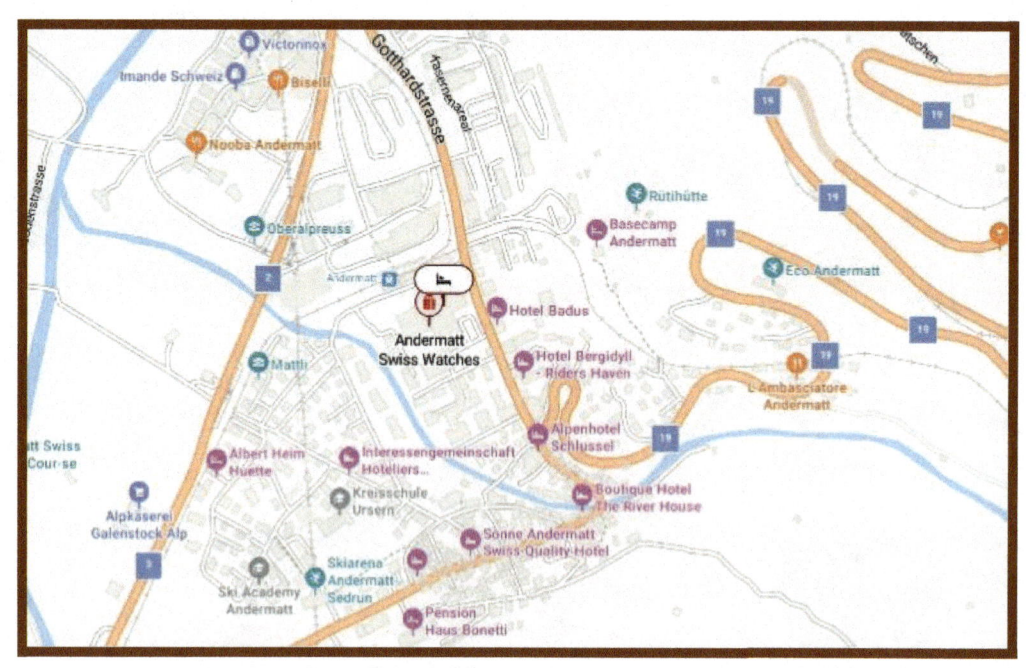

Map Showing The Chedi, Andermatt and it's Vicinity

- **Hotel Villa Honegg, Lake Lucerne** – With a famous outdoor infinity pool
  💰 From CHF 850/night
  🔗 www.villahonegg.ch

- **Beau-Rivage Palace, Lausanne** – Lakeside elegance since 1861
  💰 From CHF 500/night
  🔗 www.brp.ch

Beau-Rivage Palace, Lausanne

Switzerland Travel Guide 2025-2026

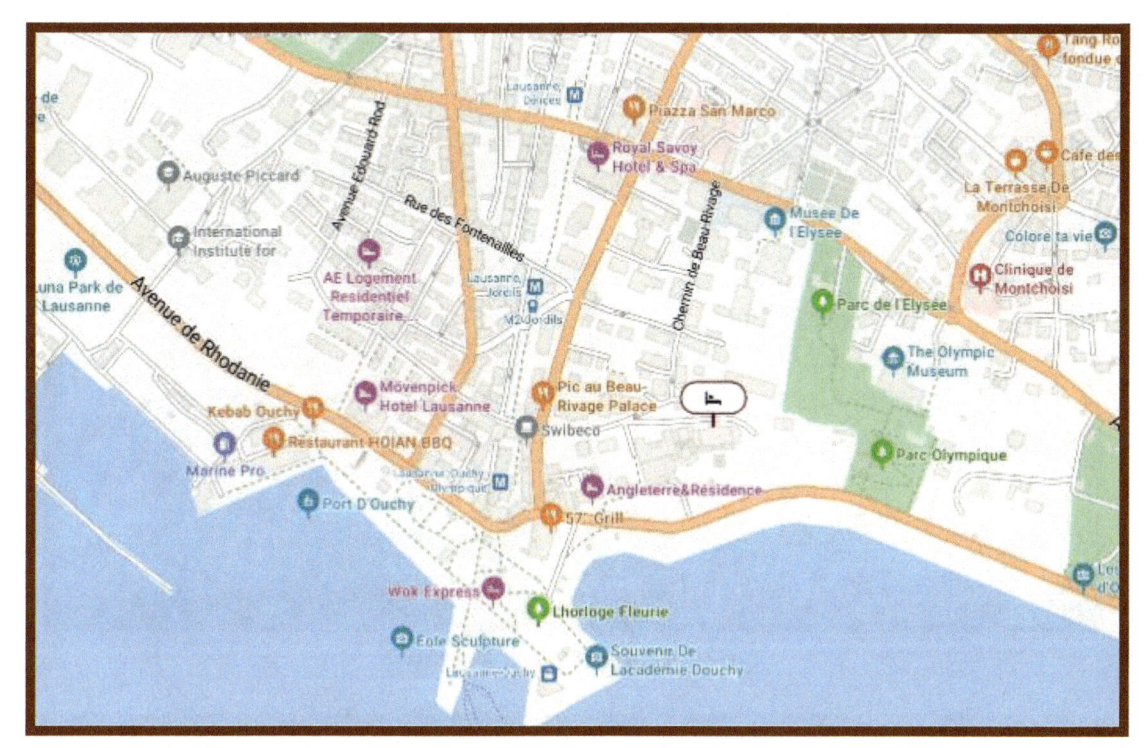

Map Showing Beau-Rivage Palace, Lausanne and it's Vicinity

🛎️ **Spa Tip:** Many luxury hotels offer **day spa access** (CHF 60–120), even if you're not staying overnight.

Family-Friendly Lodging and Group Options

Traveling with kids or in a group? Switzerland is **very family-friendly**—many hotels offer **connecting rooms, free stays for children under 6**, and amenities like bunk beds and play zones.

🎒 **Top Family Picks:**

- **Rocksresort, Laax** – Design-forward apartments near ski slopes
  💰 From CHF 190/night (2-bedroom unit)
  🔗 www.rocksresort.com
- **Swiss Youth Hostels (nationwide)** – Great family rooms, breakfast included
  🔗 www.youthhostel.ch
- **Alpen Resort Hotel, Zermatt** – Family rooms + kids' activities
  💰 From CHF 220/night
  🔗 www.alpenresort.com

Switzerland Travel Guide 2025-2026

Alpen Resort Hotel, Zermatt

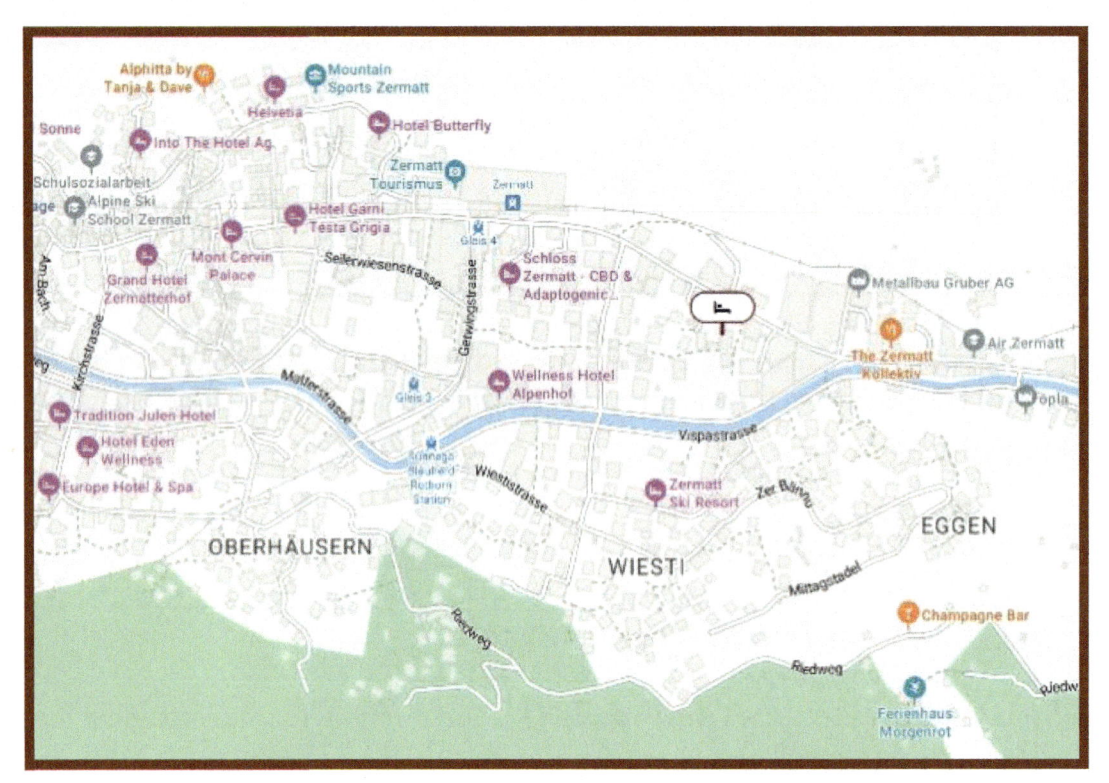

Map Showing Alpen Resort Hotel and it's Vicinity

- **Ferienart Resort & Spa, Saas-Fee** – All-inclusive family packages
  🔗 www.ferienart.ch

Switzerland Travel Guide 2025-2026

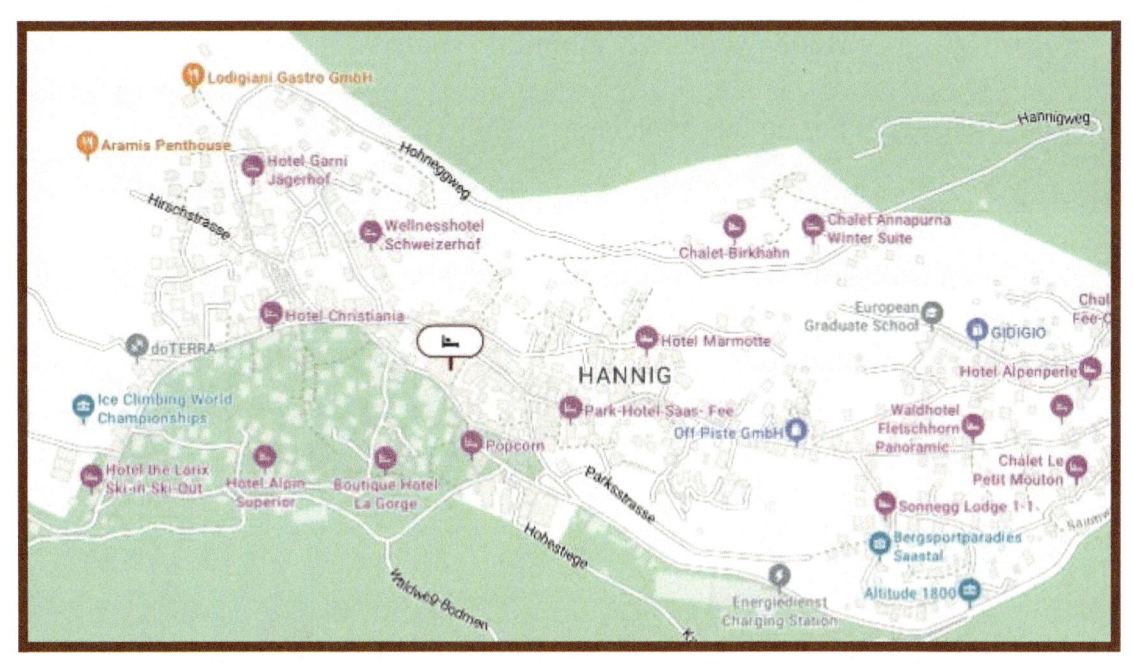

Map Showing Ferienart Resort & Spa, Saas-Fee and it's Vicinity

🛏 **Group Tip:** Book chalets or whole apartments via **e-domizil.ch** or **Interhome.ch** for better rates per person.

Booking Tips, Local Platforms, and Hidden Gems

Switzerland rewards travelers who book smart and early. Here's how to **save money** and **find special stays**.

📘 **Best Times to Book:**

- **Summer (June–Sept):** Book 2–3 months in advance
- **Winter (Dec–March):** Book ski resorts 4–6 months ahead
- **Shoulder seasons (April–May, Oct–Nov):** Lower prices, more availability

🏛 **Trusted Booking Platforms:**

- Booking.com – Most properties, flexible cancellation
- Hotels.ch – Swiss hotel platform with verified reviews

Switzerland Travel Guide 2025-2026

- e-domizil.ch – Holiday homes & mountain chalets

- Hostelworld – For budget travelers

🟫 **Hidden Gems to Explore:**

- **Gasthof zum Sternen, Wettingen** – Switzerland's oldest inn (since 1230), cozy and under the radar
  - 💰 From CHF 120/night
  - 🔗 www.sternen-wettingen.ch

- **Whitepod Eco-Luxury Hotel, Valais** – Geodesic pods with glacier views
  - 💰 From CHF 350/night
  - 🔗 www.whitepod.com

- **La Réserve Eden au Lac, Zurich** – Boutique lakefront with Art Deco charm
  - 💰 From CHF 500/night
  - 🔗 www.lareserve-zurich.com

La Réserve Eden au Lac

🧳 **Local Tip:** Always **check cancellation policies**, especially in alpine areas where weather might change your plans.

Switzerland Travel Guide 2025-2026

CHAPTER 6: TASTE OF SWITZERLAND

Iconic Swiss Dishes You Must Try

Switzerland's food is hearty, comforting, and rooted in the Alps. Here are the **absolute must-tries** that every traveler should sample:

🧀 Fondue

Cheese Fondue with bread

Melted cheese served in a pot, eaten by dipping bread with long forks. A winter staple—and a must in the mountains.

📍 **Try it at:**
Le Dézaley, Zurich – Classic Swiss-style in a cozy wooden tavern
💰 CHF 32 per person
🔗 www.le-dezaley.ch

Switzerland Travel Guide 2025-2026

🥔 Rösti

A crispy fried potato pancake, often served with eggs, bacon or melted cheese. Originally a farmers' breakfast, now a national comfort food.

📍 **Try it at:**
Wirtshaus Taube, Lucerne – Local tavern with riverside views
💰 CHF 16–22
🔗 www.taube-luzern.ch

🥘 Zürcher Geschnetzeltes

Thinly sliced veal in a creamy white wine and mushroom sauce, traditionally served with Rösti.

📍 **Try it at:**
Kronenhalle, Zurich – Elegant institution with a rich art collection
💰 CHF 49
🔗 www.kronenhalle.com

🍫 Chocolate Mousse

Chocolate mousses topped with berries

Switzerland Travel Guide 2025-2026

Light, creamy, and often topped with local berries or nuts.

📍 **Try it at:**
Café du Centre, Geneva – Art deco café near Place du Molard
💰 CHF 12

⚫ **Älplermagronen**

Älplermagronen

Alpine macaroni with potatoes, cheese, onions, and apple sauce. An unusual combo, but surprisingly addictive.

📍 **Try it at:**
Bärestarchi, Grindelwald – Cozy mountain hut-style restaurant
💰 CHF 20–25

Best Places to Eat: Local Cafés, Markets & Restaurants

You don't need a white tablecloth to eat well in Switzerland. In fact, some of the best food is served at street stalls, farmers' markets, and lakeside cafés.

Switzerland Travel Guide 2025-2026

✒️ Local Markets

- **Bern Market (Tuesdays & Saturdays)** – Fresh produce, meats, pastries
    - 📍 Bundesplatz, Bern
    - 🔗 www.bern.com

- **Carouge Market, Geneva (Wednesdays & Saturdays)** – French-style market with artisan cheeses and local wines
    - 📍 Place du Marché, Carouge
    - 💰 Free entry

The Market square in Carouge bordering Geneva

☕ Cafés

- **Café Schober**, Zurich – Historic patisserie in Old Town
    - 💰 CHF 6–10 for pastries
    - 🔗 www.cafeschober.ch

- **Confiserie Bachmann**, Lucerne – Great for local quiches and chocolate
    - 💰 CHF 10–20 per meal
    - 🔗 www.bachmann.ch

Switzerland Travel Guide 2025-2026

🍽 Top Mid-Range Restaurants

- **Zunfthaus zur Waag**, Zurich – Beautiful old guild hall with hearty classics
    - 💰 CHF 30–50
    - 🔗 www.zunfthaus-zur-waag.ch
- **Buvette des Bains**, Geneva – Local favorite by the lake; casual, scenic
    - 💰 CHF 15–25
    - 🔗 www.buvette-bainsdespaquis.ch

Buvette des Bains

Swiss Chocolate, Cheese, and Alpine Cuisine

◆ Swiss Chocolate

Switzerland takes chocolate seriously—this is where **Lindt, Toblerone, Läderach**, and **Cailler** were born.

- **Maison Cailler**, Broc – Factory tour, tastings, and hands-on workshops
    - 💰 CHF 15 (includes samples!)
    - 🔗 www.cailler.ch

Switzerland Travel Guide 2025-2026

- **Läderach Shops** – Found in Zurich, Lucerne, Basel, and Geneva
  - 💰 CHF 6–12 for gourmet bars
  - 🔗 www.laederach.com

🧀 Swiss Cheese

Famous for **Gruyère, Emmental, Appenzeller**, and **Raclette**.

- **La Maison du Gruyère**, Gruyères – Factory with tasting room & gift shop
  - 💰 CHF 12
  - 🔗 www.lamaisondugruyere.ch

- **Raclette dinners** are best in Valais (where the dish originated) — ask for **"raclette à volonté"** (all-you-can-eat).

Close up of Raclette cheese with meats

🏔 Alpine Cuisine

Alpine restaurants often use **local dairy, cured meats, and mountain herbs**. Look for **berghotels (mountain lodges)** or **alpkäsereien (alpine dairies)** for real, rustic cooking.

Switzerland Travel Guide 2025-2026

📍 **Restaurant Aescher**, Appenzell – Famous cliffside hut, reachable by cable car + hike
💰 CHF 20–35
🔗 www.ebenalp.ch

Regional Food Specialties and Farm-to-Table Dining

Switzerland's food changes as you cross cantonal lines. Here's what to look for in each region:

🚩 **French-speaking (Romandie):**

- **Papet Vaudois** – Leek and potato mash with sausage

- **Malakoff** – Fried cheese balls (La Côte region)

Malakoff

- **Local wine** – Try a glass of **Chasselas** from Lavaux

Switzerland Travel Guide 2025-2026

🚩 **German-speaking:**

- **Basler Läckerli** – Spiced honey biscuit from Basel

Basler Läckerli

- **Berner Platte** – Mixed meats and sauerkraut

- **Nidwalden's Alpkäse** – Mountain cheese aged in caves

🚩 **Italian-speaking (Ticino):**

- **Polenta e brasato** – Slow-cooked beef with cornmeal

- **Risotto with saffron or porcini**

- **Merlot wine & chestnut desserts** (local delicacies)

🌾 **Farm-to-Table Picks**

- **Hofläden (farm shops)** – Sell cheese, honey, bread, jams directly from the source
  🔍 Find them via www.swissmilk.ch

Switzerland Travel Guide 2025-2026

- **Hofrestaurants** – Rural inns offering seasonal menus
    - *Rössli Mogelsberg* – Sustainable farm cuisine in St. Gallen
    - CHF 35–60
    - www.roessli-mogelsberg.ch

Rössli Mogelsberg

Traveler Tips: Food Safety, Allergies & Etiquette

Food Safety

- Tap water is **safe to drink**, even in mountain huts.
- Street food is clean and regulated.
- Avoid drinking **raw milk** unless clearly labeled "pasteurisiert".

⚠ Allergies & Dietary Needs

- Vegetarian and vegan options are increasingly available, especially in cities.
- Gluten-free meals can be found in most supermarkets (**Coop** and **Migros** offer labeled products).

Switzerland Travel Guide 2025-2026

- Say:
    - "Ich habe eine Nussallergie" (I have a nut allergy)
    - "Ich bin glutenfrei" (I am gluten-free)

📍 **Best for special diets:**

- **Hiltl, Zurich** – World's oldest vegetarian restaurant
  💰 CHF 25–40
  🔗 www.hiltl.ch

Hiltl Sihlpost, Zurich

🍽 **Etiquette**

- Don't start eating until someone says **"En Guete!"** (Enjoy your meal!)
- No tipping required, but rounding up or leaving **5–10%** is appreciated.
- Table service can be slow—relax, it's part of the culture.

Switzerland Travel Guide 2025-2026

CHAPTER 7: TOP DESTINATIONS & HIDDEN GEMS

Zurich, Geneva, Lucerne & Bern: Urban Highlights

■ Zurich

Switzerland's largest city blends historic charm with modern creativity.

- **Old Town (Altstadt):** Cobbled streets, ancient churches, trendy boutiques.
- **Kunsthaus Zürich:** Impressive modern and classical art
  - CHF 23
  - www.kunsthaus.ch
- **Bahnhofstrasse:** One of Europe's most elegant shopping streets.

Bahnhofstrasse, Zurich, Switzerland

Switzerland Travel Guide 2025-2026

- **Lake Zurich promenade:** Perfect for a picnic or paddleboarding.

Tip: Get the **Zurich Card** (CHF 27/day) for free transport and museum entry.
🔗 www.zuerich.com

■ Geneva

Diplomatic, international, and polished—but still scenic.

- **Jet d'Eau:** Famous fountain shooting water 140m into the air.

The Jet D'eau fountain on Lake Geneva

- **United Nations Tour:** Insight into global diplomacy.
  ■ CHF 15
  🔗 www.ungeneva.org

- **Patek Philippe Museum:** A gem for watch lovers.
  ■ CHF 10
  🔗 www.patekmuseum.com

Switzerland Travel Guide 2025-2026

Patek Philippe Museum

Tip: The **Geneva Transport Card** comes free with most hotel stays—includes buses, trams, boats.

🏛 Lucerne

Storybook town with a medieval soul.

- **Chapel Bridge (Kapellbrücke):** Iconic 14th-century wooden bridge.

- **Mt. Pilatus or Mt. Rigi:** Easily accessible day trips by cogwheel train or boat.
  🎟 Round-trip combo: CHF 72–110
  🔗 www.pilatus.ch | www.rigi.ch

- **Swiss Museum of Transport:** Great for families.
  🎟 CHF 32
  🔗 www.verkehrshaus.ch

🏰 Bern

The quiet capital with **UNESCO-protected medieval streets**.

- **Zytglogge Clock Tower:** Join the 15th-century mechanical time show.

Switzerland Travel Guide 2025-2026

Street view on Kramgasse with Zytglogge Clock Tower in the old town of Bern

- **Bear Park:** Free attraction just outside Old Town.
- **Federal Palace (Bundeshaus):** Tours available when parliament's not in session.

Tip: Use the **Bern Ticket** (free with hotel stays) for unlimited public transit.

Interlaken, Zermatt & Jungfrau: Alpine Adventures

🔺 Interlaken

Base camp for thrill-seekers.

- **Paragliding:** CHF 170–210 for a tandem jump
  🔗 www.alpinair-paragliding.com

Switzerland Travel Guide 2025-2026

- **Harder Kulm Viewpoint:** CHF 38 return, breathtaking view of Jungfrau peaks.

- **Boat ride on Lake Thun or Lake Brienz:** Scenic and calm.

◼ Zermatt

Home of the **Matterhorn** and Switzerland's best ski slopes.

- **Gornergrat Railway:** CHF 88 return without pass
  🔗 www.gornergrat.ch

- **Matterhorn Glacier Paradise:** Europe's highest cable car
  🎫 CHF 95+
  🔗 www.matterhornparadise.ch

Matterhorn Glacier Paradise

- **Village charm:** Car-free streets, horse carriages, fondue huts.

❄ Jungfrau Region

Lauterbrunnen, Grindelwald, Mürren – all postcard perfect.

Switzerland Travel Guide 2025-2026

- **Jungfraujoch – Top of Europe:** 3,454m elevation
    - CHF 104–210 depending on departure point and passes
    - www.jungfrau.ch
- **Lauterbrunnen Valley:** 72 waterfalls and fairytale trails.

Lauterbrunnen valley, Switzerland

- **Mürren & Wengen:** Traffic-free villages with epic views.

Tip: Get the **Berner Oberland Regional Pass** if spending several days here.
www.regionalpass-berneroberland.ch

Lake Geneva, Montreux & Lausanne: Lakeside Beauty

Lake Geneva (Lac Léman)

Calm, clean, and wrapped in vineyards and castles.

- **Chillon Castle:** Lakeside fortress straight out of a fantasy novel
    - CHF 13.50
    - www.chillon.ch

Switzerland Travel Guide 2025-2026

🎷 Montreux

Home of the **Montreux Jazz Festival** (early July), and a peaceful lakeside escape the rest of the year.

- **Freddie Mercury statue** and lakeside trail.

- **Rochers-de-Naye cogwheel train:** Stunning view from 2,042m
  🎟 CHF 70 round-trip
  🔗 www.goldenpass.ch

🍷 Lausanne

Aerial view of Lausanne downtown city in Switzerland

The Olympic capital and a hilltop city with energy.

- **Olympic Museum:** One of the most interactive in Europe
  🎟 CHF 20
  🔗 www.olympics.com/museum

- **Lavaux vineyards:** UNESCO site with wine tastings and panoramic walks
  🔗 www.lavaux-unesco.ch

Tip: Visit in autumn for grape harvest and golden hillsides.

Switzerland Travel Guide 2025-2026

Off-the-Beaten-Path Villages and Natural Wonders

Switzerland's best-kept secrets lie away from the crowds.

◼ Guarda (Graubünden)

Tiny Engadine village with sgraffito-painted houses and total silence.
Perfect for: Hikers, artists, and those who love slow travel.

🏠 Ernen (Valais)

Culture-rich hamlet hosting classical concerts in summer.
Stay at: Hotel Alpenblick, rooms from CHF 140
🔗 www.hotelalpenblick.ch

◖ Creux du Van (Jura Neuchâtelois)

Aerial view of Creux du Van

Switzerland's "Grand Canyon"—a 160m natural rock amphitheatre.
Hike time: 4 hours round-trip. Spot ibexes in the wild.

Switzerland Travel Guide 2025-2026

🪨 Aare Gorge (Haslital)

Walk through dramatic stone walls carved by glaciers.
🎟 CHF 10
🔗 www.aareschlucht.ch

⛰ Vals

A thermal spa village surrounded by raw mountain beauty.
Don't miss: 7132 Therme, designed by architect Peter Zumthor
🎟 Spa access from CHF 80
🔗 www.7132.com

Fantastic View To A Summit In Vals In Switzerland

UNESCO World Heritage Sites in Switzerland

Switzerland has **12 UNESCO-listed sites**, and each one reveals a unique piece of the country's identity.

🏛 Old Town of Bern

Medieval arcades, fountains, and sandstone buildings frozen in time.
Free to explore, guided tours available at the tourist office.

Switzerland Travel Guide 2025-2026

🚂 Rhaetian Railway in the Albula/Bernina Landscapes

The track itself is the star. Ride the **Bernina Express** for sweeping glacier views.
🔗 www.rhb.ch

🍇 Lavaux Vineyard Terraces

800-year-old terraced wine slopes above Lake Geneva. Perfect for walking, sipping, and photographing.
🔗 www.lavaux-unesco.ch

🚶 Swiss Alps Jungfrau-Aletsch

A pristine alpine world with glaciers, rare flora, and endless trails.
Start from **Fiesch, Bettmeralp or Lauterbrunnen**.

🏰 Abbey of St. Gall

Aerial view of Abbey of St Gall and old town of St Gallen at sunrise

A baroque masterpiece with a library that looks like Hogwarts.
🎟 CHF 18
🔗 www.stibi.ch

Switzerland Travel Guide 2025-2026

CHAPTER 8: SMART TRAVEL TOOLS

Must-Have Travel Apps for Switzerland

Traveling through Switzerland becomes **effortless with the right apps**. Here are the essentials that work even offline or with limited signal in the Alps.

🔋 SBB Mobile (Swiss Federal Railways)

Your best friend for real-time train, tram, and bus schedules.

- Plan, buy and store tickets
- See platform changes instantly
  🔗 www.sbb.ch/en
  💡 **Tip:** Works in multiple languages; save your routes to avoid last-minute confusion.

📕 Swiss Travel Guide (by Switzerland Tourism)

Official destination guide with **local tips, maps, and hidden spots** by region. Works offline.
🔗 www.myswitzerland.com

☀ MeteoSwiss

Accurate, hyperlocal Swiss weather forecasts—including mountain passes, ski conditions, and avalanche warnings.
🔗 www.meteoswiss.admin.ch

🥾 Komoot or AllTrails

Great for finding and downloading **hiking, biking, and snowshoe routes** with distance, elevation, and trail reviews.
🔗 www.komoot.com | www.alltrails.com

🗣 SayHi Translate

Switzerland Travel Guide 2025-2026

Real-time voice translator that works well for **German, French, Italian, and Romansh**. Offline mode available.
🔗 www.sayhi.com

SIM Cards, Roaming, and Wi-Fi Access

⬛ Prepaid SIM Cards

Available at Zurich, Geneva, and Basel airports, major train stations, and convenience stores like **k kiosk** or **Swisscom** shops.

Swisscom store in the town of Winterthur

- **Swisscom Prepaid** – Strongest coverage, especially in rural areas
   💰 CHF 20–30 for SIM + 3GB data
   🔗 www.swisscom.ch
- **Sunrise Prepaid** – Great city coverage, solid value
   💰 CHF 19.90 for SIM + 5GB
   🔗 www.sunrise.ch
- **Salt Mobile** – Budget option, better for city-only travel
   💰 CHF 15 for SIM + 2GB
   🔗 www.salt.ch

Switzerland Travel Guide 2025-2026

Tip: You'll need your **passport** to register a SIM in Switzerland.

▌ Roaming

EU visitors can often roam at no extra charge. Non-EU travelers should check with their home carrier—roaming charges can be high.

▌ Wi-Fi Access

- Free Wi-Fi is available at major train stations, airports, McDonald's, Starbucks, and hotels.

McDonald's Barfüsserplatz, Basel, Switzerland

- In cities, **"FreeWifi SBB"** is offered at most rail hubs.

Emergency Contacts & Useful Swiss Helplines

▌ Emergency Numbers

- **Police: 117**
- **Fire: 118**
- **Ambulance: 144**
- **Pan-European emergency: 112**

Switzerland Travel Guide 2025-2026

🧳 Traveler Support

- **Swiss Travel Hotline (Multilingual):**
  📞 +41 848 100 200
  🔗 www.myswitzerland.com

REGA Swiss Air-Rescue on stand-by at Bern-Belp airport. Bern, Switzerlan

- **Rega (Air Rescue, if hiking/skiing):**
  📞 1414 or via **Rega app**
  🔗 www.rega.ch

- **Embassy Directory:** For lost passports or legal help
  🔗 www.eda.admin.ch

Tip: Always save your **passport number, insurance details, and emergency contact** in your phone and carry a printed copy too.

Currency Converters, Train Schedulers & Translators

💱 Currency Converters

Switzerland Travel Guide 2025-2026

- **XE Currency** – Live CHF conversions
  - 🔗 www.xe.com
- **Wise App** – Great if you're using their travel card
  - 🔗 www.wise.com

📱 Train Schedulers

- **SBB Mobile** (again!) – Real-time train and tram schedules
- **Rail Planner App** – For those using a **Eurail or Interrail pass**

🗣 Language Help

- **Deepl Translator** – Better nuance than Google Translate
  - 🔗 www.deepl.com

Tip: Always keep **offline translations** handy when hiking, especially in remote Romansh-speaking areas.

Tech Travel Tips: Charging, Adapters & Connectivity

🔌 Plugs and Voltage

- Plug type: **Type J (Swiss-specific)** – two or three prongs
- Voltage: **230V / 50Hz**
- Bring a **universal adapter** (or Swiss-specific one if you want a perfect fit)

🔋 Power Banks

Useful for long scenic train rides or when hiking. Look for **10,000mAh+ capacity**. Most hotels don't provide USB outlets by default.

💡 Connectivity Tips

- **Hotels and cafés** often require a code to access Wi-Fi; ask at the counter.
- **Mountain huts and remote villages** may have limited or no signal—download **offline maps** in advance.
- **Cable car stations** usually have signal, even at high altitudes.

Bonus Tip: Use **Airplane Mode** while using GPS—it saves battery and still tracks your location if maps are downloaded.

Switzerland Travel Guide 2025-2026

CHAPTER 9: STAYING SAFE, CLEAN & INFORMED

Hygiene Standards and Public Facilities

Switzerland sets the bar high when it comes to cleanliness. Public spaces are well-maintained and **littering is socially unacceptable**.

🚽 Public Toilets

- Found at **train stations, major tourist sites, city centers, and hiking trailheads**.
- Most are clean, modern, and **self-cleaning units** are common.
- Many are free, but in busy cities like Zurich or Lucerne, you may pay **CHF 1–2**.

📍 Zurich HB (main station): Public restrooms, coin or card-operated.
📍 Bern: Clean, free toilets around Bundesplatz and the station.

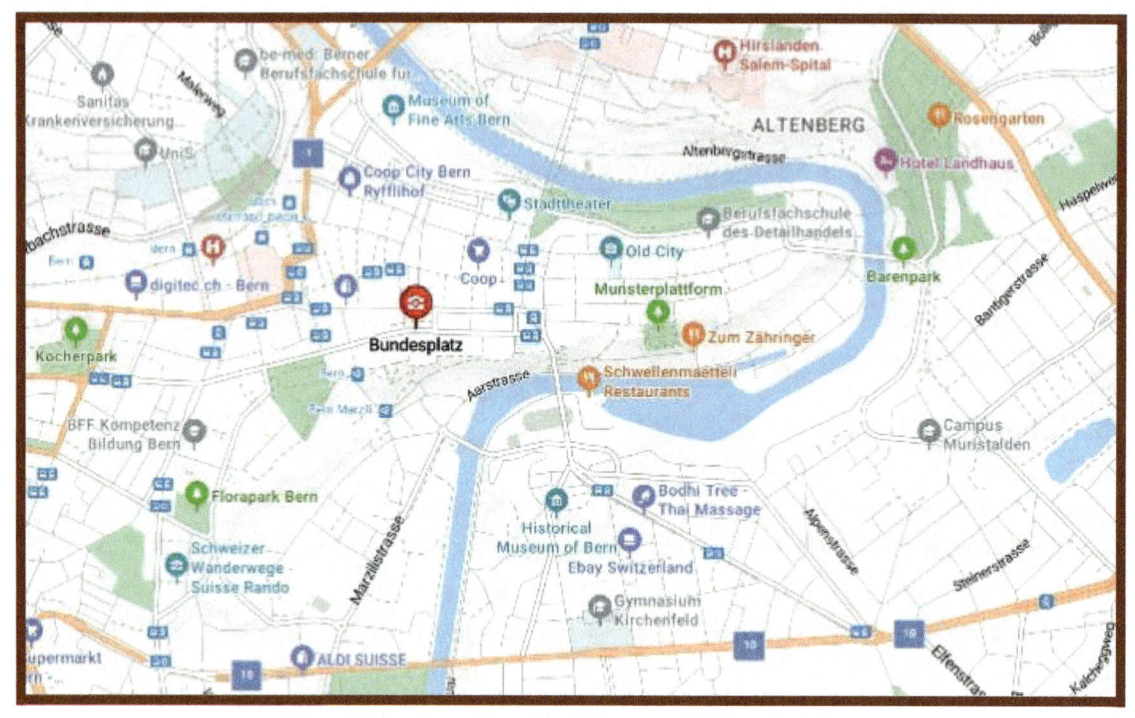

Map Showing Bundesplatz and it's Vicinity

Switzerland Travel Guide 2025-2026

🍫 Hygiene Tips

- Carry **hand sanitizer** in rural or mountain areas.
- **Tap water is drinkable everywhere**, including alpine fountains.
- **Waste bins are everywhere**—sort your trash (recyclables, paper, general waste).

🍫 **Tip:** Use apps like **Toilet Finder** or **WC Finder** for public restroom locations.

Healthcare Access and Emergency Services

Switzerland has world-class healthcare, but it's expensive without insurance.

🏥 Hospitals & Clinics

- Emergency care is available to everyone, but expect to **pay upfront** without coverage.
- Pharmacies (marked **"Apotheke"** in German areas) provide **basic treatments and advice**.

Apotheke, Bern, Switzerland

Switzerland Travel Guide 2025-2026

- **Hospital emergency rooms** are available in all major cities (University Hospital Zurich, Hôpital de la Tour Geneva, Inselspital Bern).

University Hospital Zurich

📞 **In an emergency:**

- **Ambulance: 144**

- **General emergency (EU standard): 112**

💊 **Pharmacy Tip**

- Pharmacists are highly trained and can assist with **non-life-threatening issues** (colds, allergies, altitude sickness).

- **Pharmacies are closed on Sundays**, but emergency ones rotate duty—check notices on doors or visit 🔗 www.pharmnet.ch

📓 **Travel Insurance Reminder:** Ensure your policy covers **medical, evacuation, and sports-related accidents**, especially if skiing or hiking.

Switzerland Travel Guide 2025-2026

Travel Safety Tips and Common Laws to Know

Switzerland is one of the **safest countries in the world**, but that doesn't mean you should let your guard down.

■ General Safety

- Violent crime is **extremely rare**.

- **Pickpocketing** happens occasionally in crowded areas (e.g. train stations in Geneva or Zurich).

Map Showing Geneva and it's Vicinity

- **Night travel is safe**, including trams and trains—but stay aware and avoid dark, isolated areas.

⚖ Key Laws Every Traveler Should Know

- **Jaywalking is illegal** and fined on the spot—cross only at marked areas.

Switzerland Travel Guide 2025-2026

- **Public transport fines** are steep (CHF 100+) if caught without a valid ticket.

- **Quiet hours** apply in residential areas (typically **10pm–6am**)—avoid loud music or talking on balconies.

- **Cannabis is decriminalized in small amounts** but not fully legal—don't carry or smoke it in public.

💬 **Tip:** Always carry your **passport or a copy**—Swiss police can ask for ID at any time.

Travel Scams to Avoid and How to Report Issues

Switzerland isn't known for scams, but like anywhere, **tourist-heavy zones** can attract petty tricks.

🕵 Scams to Watch Out For

- **Fake charity petitions:** Often near stations—ignore and walk on.

- **Overpriced taxis:** Use official taxi apps or **Uber** in cities like Zurich and Geneva.

- **Street performers with a "fee":** Watching is free; don't feel pressured to tip unless you want to.

📞 Reporting Issues

- **Lost property:** Report to the **nearest train station's Lost & Found** or online via SBB's lost item system
  🔗 www.sbb.ch/en/lost

- **Non-emergency police matters:**
  📞 Call **117**, or visit a local police station.

💬 **Tip:** Keep photos of valuables and your passport in cloud storage in case of loss or theft.

Switzerland Travel Guide 2025-2026

Respecting Nature: Environmental Responsibility

Switzerland is famous for its pristine landscapes, and locals take environmental care seriously.

🌿 **Leave No Trace**

- **Pack out everything** you bring into the mountains.

- Stay on **marked trails** to avoid damaging delicate alpine flora.

- **Don't pick wildflowers**, especially protected ones like Edelweiss.

Edelweiss Flower

● **Recycling is a National Habit**

- Sort waste into:

    - **PET bottles**

    - **Aluminium & tins**

Switzerland Travel Guide 2025-2026

- - **Paper**
  - **Glass**
- Use labelled bins at stations, grocery stores, and trailheads.

🚲 Eco-Friendly Travel

- Rent an **e-bike or regular bike** for short distances (PubliBike from CHF 0.25/min).
  🔗 www.publibike.ch

Publibike Zurich

- **Public transport runs on hydroelectric power**—a green choice from city to summit.

📍 **Swiss Parks App** helps you find low-impact trails, eco-accommodation, and regional conservation tips.
🔗 www.parks.swiss

💬 **Tip:** If hiking in cattle zones, always **close gates**, keep dogs leashed, and **don't approach grazing animals**—especially mother cows.

Switzerland Travel Guide 2025-2026

CHAPTER 10: LIFE IN MOTION – SPORTS & MODERN SWITZERLAND

Popular Sports and Outdoor Activities

Switzerland lives and breathes the outdoors. No matter the season, there's **something active to do**, and locals make movement a way of life.

🎿 Winter Sports

- **Skiing & Snowboarding** – The Alps offer everything from beginner hills to Olympic-level runs.
    Top resorts:
    - **Zermatt** (Matterhorn paradise)

Switzerland Travel Guide 2025-2026

- **St. Moritz** (luxury and long runs)

- **Laax** (snowboarding haven)
  - Lift passes: CHF 55–85/day
  - www.myswitzerland.com/winter

- **Snowshoeing & Winter Hiking** – Well-marked trails in regions like **Engadine** and **Jura**.

Rocky cliff with snow, and green grass in Jura mountain

🚴 Summer Adventures

- **Hiking** – Over **65,000km of marked trails**, many with views that'll stop you in your tracks.
  Start with:

  - **The Five Lakes Walk (Zermatt)**
  - **Lauterbrunnen to Mürren**
  - **Creux du Van, Neuchâtel**
    Download trails on the **SwissMobility app**
    www.schweizmobil.ch

Switzerland Travel Guide 2025-2026

- **Cycling** – Dedicated long-distance routes like **Route 9 (Lakes Route)** or **Route 1 (Rhone Route)**.
  Rent bikes at stations via **Rent a Bike**
    - 💰 CHF 30–50/day
    - 🔗 www.rentabike.ch

🧗 Other Activities

- **Paragliding in Interlaken** – Soar over lakes and valleys
    - 💰 CHF 170–220 for tandem flights
    - 🔗 www.skywings.ch

- **Via Ferrata** – Safe but thrilling mountain climbing routes with steel cables and ladders (e.g., **Mürren–Gimmelwald**).

Climbers crossing river on via ferrata

Current Events and Local Happenings (2025–2026)

Switzerland's calendar is full of **seasonal festivals, cultural traditions, and international showcases**.

Switzerland Travel Guide 2025-2026

🎭 Not-to-Miss Events

- **Montreux Jazz Festival (July 2025 & 2026)**
  One of the best in Europe, right by Lake Geneva
  🎟 Free lakeside shows; big names CHF 60–250
  🔗 www.montreuxjazzfestival.com

- **Fête de l'Escalade (Geneva, Dec 2025)**
  A lively medieval celebration with torches, soup pots, and parades.

- **Locarno Film Festival (August)** – Switzerland's answer to Cannes.
  🎟 CHF 15–40 per screening
  🔗 www.locarnofestival.ch

🎞 Current Trends

- **Sustainable tourism** is a major national focus. Expect more **eco-certified hotels, green rail packages**, and **low-impact activities**.
- Cities like **Zurich** and **Lausanne** continue leading in **urban design, bike culture**, and **digital services**.

Swiss Innovation and Modern Lifestyle

Switzerland isn't just old towns and cheese—it's also on the **cutting edge of clean tech, finance, design, and research**.

🔬 Innovation Hotspots

- **Zurich** – Home to ETH Zurich (where Einstein studied) and a hub for AI, robotics, and biotech startups.
  Visit the **Technopark** or **Museum of Digital Art (MuDA)**
  🎟 CHF 10
  🔗 www.muda.co
- **Lausanne** – EPFL (Swiss Federal Institute of Technology) leads in sustainable architecture and engineering.

🎞 Modern Living

- Public services are **highly digitalized**—you'll find apps for transport, waste sorting, tax payments, and even local events.

Switzerland Travel Guide 2025-2026

- **Public transport, healthcare, and education** are often held up as world benchmarks.

- Locals balance work and leisure—don't be surprised if office hours end early on a sunny afternoon for a bike ride.

💬 **Tip:** Switzerland's work-life balance is real. Plan meetings (or visits) outside lunch (12–1:30pm), when even city life pauses.

Volunteering, Working, and Extended Stay Tips

Planning a longer stay? Switzerland has paths for **volunteers, workers, and students**, but paperwork is serious business.

👤 Working in Switzerland

- EU/EFTA citizens can work with minimal red tape.

- Non-EU citizens need a **job offer first**, and work permits are highly competitive.

- High salaries are balanced by high living costs. Zurich and Geneva regularly rank among the **world's most expensive cities**.

🔗 Info & permit guide: www.sem.admin.ch

🌱 Volunteering

- Programs in **organic farming, sustainability, and education**.

- Try:

    - **WWOOF Switzerland** – Work on farms in exchange for food + board
      🔗 www.wwoof.ch

    - **Service Civil International** – Social and environmental projects
      🔗 www.scich.org

Switzerland Travel Guide 2025-2026

🎓 Study or Long-Term Stays

- Top universities: **ETH Zurich, EPFL Lausanne, University of Geneva**

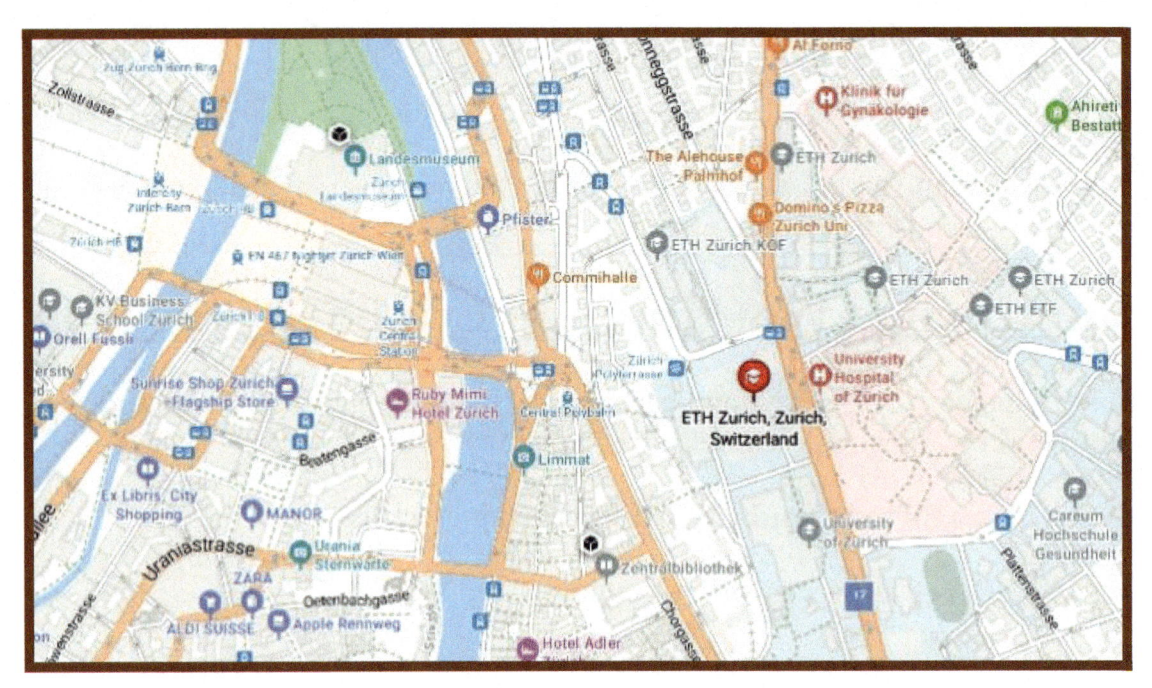

Map Showing ETH Zurich and it's Vicinity

- Student visas require **proof of funds**, **admission letter**, and **health insurance**.

📝 **Tip:** Health insurance is **mandatory for all stays over 3 months**.

Engaging with Locals: Language, Respect & Cultural Exchange

💬 Language Basics

Switzerland has **four national languages**, and English is widely spoken—but showing effort goes a long way.

- In German-speaking areas:
    - "Grüezi" – Hello

Switzerland Travel Guide 2025-2026

- - "Danke" – Thank you
  - In French-speaking areas:
    - "Bonjour" – Hello
    - "Merci" – Thank you
  - In Italian-speaking Ticino:
    - "Buongiorno" – Good day
    - "Grazie" – Thanks

📘 Use the **SayHi Translate** or **Duolingo** app for quick learning.

👤 Social Norms

- **Punctuality is everything**—being late is seen as disrespectful.
- Swiss people are **friendly but reserved**. Small talk is polite but short.
- Always **greet with a firm handshake** or three-kiss greeting (among friends).

👌 Cultural Experiences

- Join a **yodeling or alphorn workshop** in Appenzell.
- Participate in a **cheese-making session** in Gruyères or Emmental.
- Attend a **local wrestling festival (Schwingen)** in central Switzerland for a peek into traditional sport.

🔍 Find activities on:
🔗 www.myswitzerland.com

Switzerland Travel Guide 2025-2026

CONCLUSION

Traveling through Switzerland is more than ticking off a list of postcard sights. It's about **savoring melted cheese beside a roaring fireplace in a mountainside chalet, hearing the clang of cowbells echo through a foggy alpine valley**, and **marveling at the precision of a train that winds its way through glaciers as if guided by magic**. It's a place where **the wild and the polished exist in perfect balance**—where you can hike across a silent ridge in the morning and sip espresso in a cosmopolitan art gallery that same afternoon.

What makes Switzerland special isn't just its scenery—it's **the ease, elegance, and quiet confidence** with which it welcomes the world. Whether you're traveling solo with a backpack, with loved ones in tow, or indulging in five-star luxury, the country wraps you in a sense of calm that's hard to find elsewhere. And once you feel it—you'll understand why **people don't just visit Switzerland, they return**.

As you close this guide and begin dreaming, planning, or even packing, remember this: **you don't have to see it all to be moved by Switzerland.** Sometimes it's the quietest moments that stay with you—the sound of boots crunching fresh snow, the first sip of hot chocolate after a lakeside walk, or a friendly "Grüezi!" from someone on a winding village trail.

So whether your journey leads you through bustling Zurich, up the icy heights of Jungfrau, into the vineyard-lined roads of Lavaux, or toward the hidden corners of Ticino and Graubünden, know that you're stepping into a country that rewards **curiosity, care, and open-hearted travel**.

Switzerland may be small, but what it offers is immense: **clean air, safe streets, deep traditions, modern brilliance, and a touch of wonder around every corner**.

This isn't the end—this is your invitation. Your story in Switzerland is waiting to be written. Let it be full of discovery, delight, and memories worth sharing again and again.

Bon voyage. Gute Reise. Buon viaggio. Bun viadi.

Switzerland is ready for you.

Switzerland Travel Guide 2025-2026

Printed in Dunstable, United Kingdom